Sumthin' T' Say

Poems and Essays on Everyday Situations

By Rose Jackson-Beavers

P.O. Box 2535
Florissant, Mo 63033

Edited by: Terra Little
Photographer: Marquis Mann
Models: Adeesha Beavers
Cover Designed by Sheldon Mitchell of Majaluk

Manufactured in the United States of America

ISBN 13: 9780981648323
ISBN 10: 0-9816483-2-0

Library of Congress Control Number: 2008928810

For information regarding discounts for bulk purchases, please contact Prioritybooks Publications at
1-314-306-2972 or rosebeav03@yahoo.com

Sumthin' T' Say

Poems and Essays on Everyday Situations

Published by Prioritybooks Publications

Other books by Rose Jackson-Beavers

Quilt Designs and Poetry Rhymes
Backroom Confessions
A Hole in My Heart

TABLE OF CONTENTS

DEDICATION

I dedicate this book to all the people who touched my life in a profound and memorable way.

To my parents, L.J. (Bo) and Connie Mae, who led by example and helped me achieve my greatest dream by showing their love and support of all my endeavors. Thank you both for allowing me to dream and for making my dreams come true.

To my husband and best friend, Cedric, for your loving support and trust. To my daughter, Adeesha, for whom I do all that I do. You were my dream come true. I love you both.

To my cousin, Maxine March, for proving that God works miracles for those who believe.

To my late brother, McKinley Jackson, for your love and leadership.

ACKNOWLEDGMENTS

There are so many people whom I call friends, supporters, and inspirations, because they encouraged me when I didn't want to be encouraged. They saw something in my life that glittered. I want to thank each of you for being in my corner, because if it were not for you I would not have been able to put my feelings on paper and believe that others would enjoy what I had to say. I thank you, Edna Patterson-Petty, a well-known artist who many times promoted me when you should or could have promoted yourself. Thank you for pushing me and others when we said, "I always wanted to do this, but..." To that you simply responded, "Do it now!" and found resources and other avenues to help us stop making excuses and try. *Sumthin' T' Say* exemplifies you, because you always have something to say whenever you discover the dreams of others.

To Mrs. Johnnie Penelton, my former supervisor, friend and Delta Sigma Theta Sorority sister, for giving me blessings to succeed, believing I could do the things that seemed impossible and for giving me another great person to look up to and admire. Thank you for starting the Circle of Friends Book Club, where I first read and shared my poems, using them as props from a book we were reading.

To the Circle of Friends founding members: Mary Tomlin, whom I read poems to over the phone; Rose Mary Tally, my ace in the hole, salesperson and special motivator; Julie Penelton, who always wanted to read 1,000-page books; Marcia Moore, my editor and main supporter; Melony Thomas, a great cook and intriguing lady; Cheryl Little Berry, who made my Mondays happy with her positive attitude; Vikki Collier, who has read much of my work during the years I've known you; Steve Hall, a poet himself and a great friend; Kelvin Ellis, for encouraging me to write; and Lillie Tate, a long time co-worker, a great listener. Thank you, Telia Starks and Margaret Mandley, for reading my work in its infancy.

Thanks to George Cotton, aka "The Great Inspirator," for giving me my first column as a freelance writer, and Amagazine and its creators for being positive African-American men who had a dream and pursued it. Thank you, Ms. Mary R. Rhodes, who is also a sorority sister, for giving me my first poetry book.

There are so many other people who have encouraged me for so many years and to them I would also like to say thank you: My dear late brother, McKinley, for supporting me financially, giving me valuable advice while I was in college and giving me much love all my life. My brother Chester (Felinda), my late brother Sylvester and Johnaver, and Sylvia Pearson, for being in my life. My sister Regina, her husband Osmund, my lil' sister Charlotte (Princess), her husband Donald and (I didn't forget you) Alfreda Marcus. Glorina (Neicy), Ms. Hudson and all my aunts—the late Zelma, Vera, and Barbara Ray. My cousins, Sally, Tracy and Joyce Ann, for being in my life. I love you guys. The Almighty for blessing me with a wonderful life, health, family, great friends and for giving me the desire to write. My nephews, Edward, Cameron, Donovan, Carlton, Jasper, Kendrick, Chester, Jr. (Slug), Terence, and Shawan (T-Man). My cousin, Timothy Jerome Jackson—choose your friends wisely and find ones who will help you grow into a positive young man.

My nieces, Melonitria, Kendrina, Nikina, Tanya, Cynthia and LeNeshia—please know that you can always dream big and reach wide, because all things are possible if you believe in God. Don't ever give up; always strive for success. And finally, to my number one aces from New Jerusalem S.D.A. Church—Elder Archie Suggs, Elder Joseph Hoyle and Sister Geretta Bonner. Also, my best friend, Mary Ann Stallworth, for being the person I could call when I needed a friend, and my walking buddy, Josephine Wren. To Soror Katie Wright, for the valuable information, and to my second family, the McClungs of Itta Bena, Mississippi, for accepting me into your lives with love and respect. You will never know how much your unconditional love has strengthened me in spirit and great determination. For those whom I may have missed acknowledging, thank you, thank you and thank you. Your support has been tremendous.

FOREWORD

Sumthin' T' Say is the result of a unique collection of modern day poems and essays with a zing. The author, Rose Jackson-Beavers, has created a funny and breezy work, of words that keep the reader in awe, while guessing what is coming next. Her use of straightforward, slangy, and colloquial language gives great emphasis on the way Rose discusses topics like relationships, love, pain and family. Most of all she writes about *YOU*.

Rose, you have shown a unique ability to reach inside all of us and share what you've discovered with words. Your talent is a blessing. This work proves you are a gifted writer, who possesses a passion for entertaining. We know that you've always got *Sumthin' T' Say*.

Telia E. Starks, Friend

DID I?

Did I do that? Write that poem?

What about doing things, when I was born?

Did I say that? On that page, from my thoughts or from my rage?

Did I hear that? What did you say?

Step back people,   I've got Sumthin' T' Say.

FAMILY

MY BROTHERS

As an adolescent, I found it thrilling to put my ear against my brothers' bedroom door and listen as they discussed the facts of life. My ears perked up when they started their daily discussions about young women. Yes, I had three very fine, attractive brothers who excelled in sports and academia. I was a very curious and observant young person, who was smart way beyond my years. Every book or article I could get my hands on, I read with great enthusiasm. So it did not faze me when my older brothers chased me, their inquisitive sister, from their door, after finding me eavesdropping.

Whenever I put my ear against that bedroom door, I clearly heard how they felt about women. So as I matured the information I pilfered from their private conversations became invaluable. One conversation I heard centered on the kind of woman they each wanted to marry. My oldest brother was adamant about not marrying a loose woman or one who would readily sleep with him. He wanted a young woman whom he could take home to meet his mom. They called out the young ladies' names that they had slept with and seemed shocked that they had so easily given it up. I heard my brothers say, "Man, I really liked that woman until she put herself out. She probably has sex with everyone she dates. That's not cool."

Hearing my brothers discuss women so openly with each other made me realize that some men wanted easy one-night stands, but for serious and everlasting relationships they were looking for someone special. I decided I would wait before I had sex with anyone.

I did not want men laughing behind closed doors about me. My brothers discussed so much behind their door—every issue you can imagine. They were very close and they loved their family to the extreme. As I grew older, I went to my brothers for all kinds of problems I thought I was having and they surely kept me from making many mistakes. So it was no surprise to me to receive letters from my brothers while I was attending college.

In one letter I wrote to my oldest brother while he was in the military, I asked him, "How will I know if a guy really likes me?" He wrote back, "You will know by the way he treats you. Does he respect you? Does he push you to do things that may be harmful to you? Is he interested in doing things you want to do? Would he go to church with you, if you asked him?" He further suggested that I invite guys to go to church with me. This gave me a mission to look for a quality relationship.

With relationships being the way they are now, it's a wonder more people who have one-night stands are not riddled with a host of illnesses and other problems. Today you may not be lucky to survive having sex without contracting a deadly disease. People who sleep around are like an accident waiting to happen. If more people use their brakes as protection to control their sexual desires, fewer people would suffer from irresponsible behavior. I'm so glad my brothers were there to guide us, so we could make better and more informed decisions. I'm so glad my brothers cared enough about their sisters to answer our questions and to serve as information banks, to prevent many disasters. I am proudest of my oldest brother, who took the time to write me and to explain the realities of life to me.

The information I heard while listening to my brothers when I was young became invaluable to me on my road to adulthood. My brothers were always there for me and our family members, and they definitely kept us from making many painful mistakes. They always listened to me and never treated me as if I were in the way.

For their love, patience and devotion, I hope I've made them proud. I am living my dreams and I can give back to others what my brothers gave to me. Thank you for your time, love and trust, which allowed me to make decisions based on firsthand information. To my brothers, I thank you for giving me courage to say *no* to negative things that could've caused me harm and for saying *yes* when I needed you by my side. I am so grateful for having brothers.

THINKING OF YOU

I think of you so much each day.

It's like you never went away.

Your smile, your laugh, your face.

The way you say,

"Baby sis, what's up today?"

So when I see a picture of your lovely face,

I know you are at rest in a peaceful place.

Dedicated to my favorite person. My oldest brother...

McKinley Jackson
4/25/55 - 7/22/95

MY BROTHERS

My brothers told me,

that I could be,

anything I thought I

could foresee.

Please yourself,

they would say.

Doing something you love

will go a long way!

BROTHERS

When we were young we had so much fun.

Playing games like,

Stop 'N Go,

Mother May I and

Simon Says.

But growing older,

my brothers changed to watching us,

with balls and chains.

They wouldn't let us girls do anything,

because in their minds we had changed,

from little girls with curls,

into young women we became.

A REASON TO SMILE

Everyday we think of you,

No matter where we go,

Or what we say and do.

We miss the time we spent together,

No matter what day or the weather.

The love you gave us made us feel special.

It gave us a reason to smile.

It made us feel better.

We miss hearing your voice, telling us as you always did,

I love my family and I always will.

To lose you as a brother,

What could be worse?

The loss of a child from his mother!

God called you home,

Because your time had come.

He wanted you because you, too, were his son.

He took you to a place where there is no sickness or pain.

He knew if he took you so full of love, family and friends,

To a place like heaven, we would all want to get in!

McKinley, we thank God everyday for giving us a brother,

A person just like you, for there could be no other.

UNITY

UNITY AMONG WOMEN

I have often heard from others about how difficult it is to work around women in any capacity. It is usually said that we cannot get along, regardless of what we say or do. Yet in many ways I refused to believe it. Based on the relationships I have shared, which include three sisters, mothers, aunts and close girlfriends, no matter how angry we made each other we always supported one another in our personal endeavors. We never encountered any problems that could not be resolved.

I know there comes a time in each of our lives when we participate in destructive conversations about someone else. For me, whenever I participate in a gossip session with others, I feel a certain level of guilt. During the times when I have said something I wish I could take back, I have tried to do something to help that person change the problem area that was discussed. For example, I have always found a way to help individuals that I have said something negative about make positive changes.

Since I am trying to be a better person, I have started practicing the art of making positive statements. When someone comes to me to talk about another person negatively, I say, "Maybe you should speak to that person," or something like, "Do you think the person knows you feel that way? Maybe you should talk to them?" I am now beginning to communicate positively and more openly with women.

I have grown a lot and I feel that, if women could better communicate with each other, we would be able to share our feelings and opinions openly. We would also be able to negotiate and resolve our differences more effectively. By communicating and listening to each other we would be able to form and share better relationships.

At least, that is what I used to think. Now that I have had the opportunity to see and observe some women in action, I see things differently.

I have observed women in the workplace who share many things in common: children, job titles, and marriages. Yet anxiety, stress and confusion are consistently present. It doesn't matter where you go, shopping, church, or to the movies, women can be heard gossiping, putting each other down, threatening to fight each other, taking each other's husbands, backstabbing on and off the job, cat fighting, and sabotaging each other. Women will give each other praise for successful work and then turn right around and laugh about what they said.

Are we women so pretentious that we can't give credit where it is due? At work, if one is given credit for spearheading successes that benefit all and is recognized for doing so, disenchantment begins. What about me? She didn't do anything special. I never get recognized for things I do. She must be the favorite, her pet or maybe a relative. Why can't she just be good at her job? If each of us works hard and becomes successful in our jobs, we will be recognized by our supervisors and peers, especially, if we are seen as team players.

Recognition may not be verbal, but it comes in many forms, such as increases in salary, job changes due to promotions or reassignments, better benefits, educational opportunities, flexible schedules, or more tools and supplies.

Eventually everyone will get their fifteen minutes of fame. Rather than being seen as someone who is envious and non-supportive of others, let us all give credit where it is due. If we can participate in upholding each other by giving positive accolades no matter what the person did, small or large, we will have opened our minds and we will be able to see our own rewards.

For me, each time a sister becomes successful it gives me the courage to move one step closer to my goals. When we make improvements in our lives we should begin supporting other women in opening businesses or any endeavor, by encouraging ourselves and others to spend our dollars in their stores. When we begin supporting each other positively, then and only then will women be able to praise each other and mean it. As for me,

I am already beginning to change for the better.

Previously Published by "AMAGAZINE"

UNITY AMONG WOMEN

Unity among women?

I don't think so.

The minute you do something great,

Your friends, they can't take.

They'll mistreat and deceive you,

do everything they can out of the blue,

To outdo and put you in a catch-22.

From looking for dirt,

To being a flirt with your man,

They'll do all they can,

To bring you to your knees,

And change all your marriage plans.

The girl and the man,

They'll make you want to disgrace them,

By having you act like a caveman.

Don't be violent or act like a madman,

Be respectful and call the lawman.

Unity Among Women?

I don't think so!

See them women coming,

You better gather up all your things,

and move your family to Beijing!

WEIGHT

FAT DAYS

Everyone always seems to be looking toward the dawn of a New Year for so many different changes to occur in their lives and in the world. Many of us have even made New Year's resolutions to change our lives in a variety of ways, such as becoming healthier, quitting smoking or losing weight. For me, weight is a difficult topic to get away from because conversations or other related events regarding weight is discussed daily.

Every time you turn on the television you hear about new diets, better exercise equipment, low-calorie or fat-free foods that are being marketed to the fat population. Not only that, but you hear about skinny models who are making millions and, finally, you hear that obesity is a national health concern. With all this attention being focused on our bodies, no wonder the diet industry is making millions by feeding off of the desire to be thin.

Pressure to be thin is an ongoing theme for many women. The media is a powerful source of hypnosis. If they say something repeatedly and we continue to hear it, we will believe it. Daily brainwashing venues include television, magazines, and clothing advertisements. Overweight people can't ignore the constant badgering, no matter how hard they try.

Loved ones are not immune to the constant barrage of information, either. They interpret the media's "diet blitz" as if they must save you, despite your feelings. Loved ones say you need to lose weight or that, if you stop eating so much, maybe you'll lose weight.

Too bad no one checked to see if you had a health problem or if you were just simply tired. Yes, you are tired of diets that don't work. You've tried everything, without success and now you are faced with fat days.

What are fat days? Fat Days are when you look in the mirror and you don't like what you see; the weight or the way your clothes fit, because nothing you put on looks good. The image in the mirror shouts out that you need to change clothes, because you look too fat in that outfit. You immediately take off the outfit you have on and run to the closet to find something more appealing. Finally, you find another outfit and to your dismay, it's just as bad.

Now your self esteem is decreasing at an incredible rate and you begin to pity yourself. "Why me?" you cry. You feel horrible as you change clothes repeatedly. Nothing looks good today, so you decide to wear the outfit you wore last week and you put it on. For now, you are okay.

You look around and see that your bedroom looks as if a tornado passed through it. Clothes are everywhere. You have spent too much time getting ready to leave the house, and now there is no more time to clean up your mess. So you leave home to start your workday and, for now, you have forgotten about your fat day. The day goes by quickly while working and finally it is time to go home. You think about all the clothes thrown around your room and think, "I'll hang them up when I get home."

Upon your return home, your spouse or another family member greets you. They ask what happened this morning, if you were having a fat day? You laugh because everyone knows your pattern. You again resolve, "No more fat days for me. I am going on a diet and I will lose this weight. I'm going to start tomorrow."

NOT FAT

I'm not fat,

Just big boned.

I'm not fat.

Shut up and leave me alone.

You never asked,

If I was sick or had an eating disorder.

You never asked,

Why I looked like that!

So why you call me fat,

Behind my back?

When all you had to do,

Was leave me alone.

No, I'm not fat,

So stay off my damn back.

DIET

No diet for me,

They don't work.

I'll learn to eat right,

And try not to take a bite,

Of all the foods that excite and delight.

Diets don't work,

Look at me

I've been on every diet,

From A to Z.

PATIENCE

PATIENCE...MEN HAVE NOT!

The other day I sat back and watched my husband teach our daughter how to work out a difficult math problem. Upon first glance, I felt proud to have a husband who cares about his daughter and is at home, willing and able to support her in understanding homework assignments and any other life issues that may present themselves. It was a joy to see them busy, working and talking over her current assignment—Algebra.

Initially, he was demonstrating the procedure for doing a particular problem and you could see the two of them conferring and sharing information. However, I noticed that the longer I watched, the more impatient he became. Apparently, my daughter was having a difficult time comprehending the concept of this particular lesson. It was an advance algebra problem and she was slow to understand.

Suddenly, his patience was shorter and he was becoming frustrated. "Why don't you understand? It's simple and I've already explained it to you three times. What are you doing?" he screamed.

Finally, I stepped in to remind him that she was only eleven years old and what seemed simple to him with his college degrees and all, wouldn't be simple to her. He took some time to try and calm down so he could be more patient as she attempted to compute the answer.

After spending time with the two, I called a close friend and before we could begin a conversation, I heard a loud, booming voice in the background. She explained that her husband was teaching their son math and he was losing patience because their son didn't seem to understand. As I waited for her to come back to the phone after talking to her husband, I thought about fathers and homework. I noted one thing: Fathers are like mothers in wanting their children to be bright, articulate and self-sufficient. When they are capable of helping them complete their homework, it gives them a feeling of pride and confidence that their children can survive in this cold world.

But when the child demonstrates a weakness that causes his mother to nurture and protect and his father to withhold privileges as punishment, this, in my opinion, is wrong. Punishing a child because they don't understand their homework could cause the child to feel that in order to please he must be perfect, thereby setting the child up for problems that could be detrimental to their emotional well-being.

I know fathers mean no harm, but I do believe that some of them have short patience and need training in controlling it. I also know that, as a parent, it is easy to lose patience with your child when you feel they are not living up to their potential. After all, we want our children to be successful and when they are not, we feel it is our fault. What did we do wrong?

While thinking about this situation, it made me evaluate men and question why they don't have more patience in other areas of their lives? You see it everyday. When they walk through the door, they want dinner cooked right now or when they see you on the phone they feel like you should be cleaning house, not wasting time gossiping. If you ask them questions they think you should know the answer to, they won't answer. But let them ask you a question and they expect an immediate answer. Do they have patience with their friends and family members? I think not, in many cases. If a family member has problems and needs their help, there is no need to explain, just say what you need and when. They'll decide whether you need something and whether you'll get it from them. The "why" is not important to most men.

Most men lack patience in other areas of their lives. For instance, what about men in traffic? You see them hitting the steering wheel, maybe using a little bit of profanity when traffic is too heavy and they feel stuck. If the car in front of them is driving too slow, they will tailgate. Watch them as they weave in and out of traffic. They don't really have anywhere to go, they just want you out of the way so they can drive nowhere fast.

Women, on the other hand, are completely different. Seldom will you find them speeding dangerously through traffic. We take our time, because we know that whoever is waiting will be there when we get there. We believe that we could possibly be in an accident when we are irrational. Not men! They don't have accidents, do they? Think about it! Women are more compassionate and willing to listen to others. They may ask a lot of questions, but they will wait patiently for the answers.

For instance, in the case of a mother helping her daughter with homework, she will look for ways to make learning fun and won't become angry when the child doesn't understand. She will go as far as calling friends and asking for strategies to help her child. When a woman is caught in traffic she will use that time to read a book, apply makeup, pick up the phone to make a business call or just to think. Seldom will you see them banging angrily on the steering wheel or weaving in and out of traffic dangerously, because they are so frustrated from waiting.

In a situation where a friend or family member needs help, women will patiently discuss the situation with them and ask, "How did you get in this situation?" We want to know. A woman will help you develop a plan to make sure it won't happen again in the near future.

Women have more patience and you don't need any statistics to support this statement. If you need more proof just perform your own test. Ask a man who is not interested in you romantically to assist you in solving a problem. Watch his hand gestures and look in his eyes. What do you notice? Does he seem really interested in what you're saying? Does he seem willing to stay with you as long as you need to solve your problem or does he check his watch as if he has somewhere to go? Watch them in traffic, what are they doing? Do they seem tense, calm, upset or are they hitting the steering wheel? Now pose the same question or situation to a woman, watch her hand gestures and her eyes. What is she doing? Is she leaning forward to listen to you? Does she seem interested in what you have to say? Does she assist you in finding a resolution to the problem, maybe occasionally guiding you? Do you feel rushed when you're talking to her, like you have to hurry to finish talking or she will lose interest? Watch her in the same slow traffic. Is she putting on makeup, reading, listening to music and singing, or talking on the phone?

Perhaps when you think about it, maybe there is nothing wrong with a man being impatient, except when he is helping his child with homework assignments. Maybe, women are supposed to be patient. How else would we be able to handle so many relationship problems without giving up?

One thing is clear, and that is, I am happy my husband has the desire and heart to be home with his family and is an important part of his daughter's life. I also appreciate that he is willing to support our daughter through role modeling and showing examples of love and support to our extended family members, even when they make him angry and impatient. For me, maybe I should become less mathematically challenged and more willing to show him support by teaching him how to become a better communicator, which could possibly help him to become a better math teacher.

Men can learn a lot from women about listening and discussing many issues, while women can learn from a man's silence that all is well with family and relationships. Otherwise, would he be home?

I leave you with this question: Are men less patient than women? You be the judge. I rest my case.

Previously published by "AMAGAZINE"

PATIENCE

Patience, my brother, men have not!

When you need them to do something,

they look at their watch.

They knew they weren't busy,

when you asked them to do a favor,

Just changed their minds,

because it was hard labor.

While driving you places,

they speed a lot.

If they get a ticket, your men are hot.

They're too embarrassed to ask for directions,

because they think they are too smart for your corrections.

Weaving in and out of traffic and tailgating too,

because they have no place to go,

they're just looking for something to do.

Working with small children,

they can't seem to handle.

When problems arise men are in shambles.

Patience, they say, is a virtue to all.

When men act a fool,

my goodness, who do you call?

SELF ESTEEM

YOU

Accepting me for who I am

was always hard to do.

Then one day I met a man,

I think I'll call him, You.

You taught me how to love again,

especially me, as I am.

Stroking me with warm fuzzies,

singing to me with soft voices,

comforting me with all your might,

holding me so very tight.

You told me that you love me.

You told me that you cared.

You told me that you needed me,

as you gently stroked my hair.

The love you gave me,

made it easy to accept myself.

For who am I to deny me,

of all those things that please me?

For you were the first to love me,

Sumthin' T' Say

until I loved myself.

Thanks to you, I love me.

Thanks to you, I care.

Never again will I ever lose

confidence or faith in myself.

Rose Jackson-Beavers

TAKE YOUR TIME

Take your time,

that's all you have to do.

And everyone around would,

stop tripping with you!

Do what you need and

think you should do,

and everyone will begin to

appreciate you, too.

Respect yourself and in

a matter of time,

 your real friends will

start coming back around.

DO UNTO OTHERS

Do unto others,

as the Bible says.

Then good things will come unto you.

Do unto others.

You know that's what you should do.

That's what our folks raised us to do.

Do unto others,

as you would like them to do unto you.

Read the Bible, it's full of life's clues.

Do unto others,

as you want them to do unto you.

That's all folks, I'm telling you!

RESPECT YOURSELF

Respecting yourself,

is so easy to do.

Then all those around,

will respect you, too!

Liking yourself,

is so important to self-esteem.

Feeling positive and good about you,

should be an everyday theme.

When your heart is happy you spread joy,

 And friends and loved ones demand to be a part of your team.

A GRANNY'S LOVE

WITHOUT YOU, I COULD DO NOTHING!

You took me in when I felt lost.
You gave me a home, when I had no house.

When my parents couldn't take care of me,
You took me in and made me worry free.

I love you for so many things,
But mostly, I love you because you're my Queen!

Without you, there could be no me!
Without you, where would I be?

Your tender loving care, devotion and love,
Had to be truly sent from God above!

How could I thank you for saving my life?
And giving me love that's larger than life.

How could I thank you for so many things,
When you are such a beautiful Queen?
Without you, I could do nothing!
With you, I have everything!

Lord, what would I have done without this love?
So I'm thanking you from high above.

My granny has given me her heart and soul,
And this has made me really "whole!"

SOMEONE CARES

Feeling Lost,

Feeling Sad,

Feeling like you never had,

Someone who loves you,

Someone who cares.

A person who could possibly be your mom or dad,

But listen to this and make sure you don't miss it.

Look up to the sky and pray to be strong 'cause,

One day you'll be going home.

To someone who won't get sick because of drugs,

He'll give you lots of hugs.

His name is Jesus, I hear.

He is the best person you could ever love.

When times get hard and you become sad,

Get on your knees and pray to your dad.

Loving God above will make you glad!

A PRAYER OF THANKS

Thank you for becoming,

The person I love.

Thanking Jesus from high above,

For giving me parents who love me,

Who chose me just as sure as could be.

I love you God for being with me,

When it seemed like no one else wanted to be.

Thank you for sending me a mother and a father,

I am so glad that they wanted to bother,

With children's illnesses and homework,

And all the other childhood irks,

Which could make a sane person go berserk.

But don't forget the other children,

Whom everyone else seems to have forgotten.

Help all adopted children find someone to personally love them,

Someone who doesn't mind being a parent and a friend.

Thank you again for such wonderful folks,

Thank you, God, so very much. Amen.

DOMESTIC VIOLENCE

LOVE DOES NOT HURT!

During one hot, humid, steamy week in the month of May, in the metropolitan area, three women lost their lives at the hands of men who said they loved them. The one common thread shared was that they all were victims of abuse and had suffered some form of abuse many times before their untimely deaths. These women, believing they were loved, never realized that the words, "If I can't have you, no one else will," were in fact, as real as the pain they experienced while struggling to gain their last breath.

The FBI's most recent statistics show that about five women are killed daily by an intimate partner in domestic disputes. These deaths and many others that are discussed in the media have brought out a variety of domestic violence issues.

What is domestic violence? Domestic violence includes sexual, physical, verbal and mental abuse. Depending on how abuse is interpreted, potential victims may not be aware that they are in dangerous situations. Although hitting is the most familiar form of abuse, incidents of mental and verbal abuse are just as bad, because they lower one's self-esteem and may cause many other psychological problems for the victim.

When one thinks about verbal abuse and being called dirty, ugly and hurtful names, it brings to mind the old saying: "Sticks and stones may break my bones but words will never hurt me." Words do hurt and for many individuals these words will cause negative self-worth, as well as low self-esteem, leading victims to stay in dangerous conditions.

They believe they can't make it without their men and that no one else would want them. Thinking no one cares, they stay and take the beatings. Abuse in any form is wrong and no one should tolerate having pain inflicted on them. It is not the victim's fault the abuser doesn't know how to control his anger.

Most abuse is inflicted by those who say they love their victims. Loved ones who are feeling betrayed, lost and hurt, lash out at the one person they claim to love most, leaving surviving family members asking, "Why?"

There are so many reasons why victims stay in abusive situations, for instance:

1.   "I love him and he loves me; that's why he hits me. It's not his fault! I did something stupid."

We all have a constant need to feel loved and victims have already been brainwashed to believe that no one else would love them. So they stay, because it's comfortable and it's all they know. But in order to know love, women must first love themselves. When this happens, it will be easy for others to love them in return.

2.   "He takes care of me and keeps a roof over my head." He is doing nothing different from what women could do for themselves if they tried.

3.   "It's hard to find a man." Well, maybe it is. But is it better to have a man who keeps you riddled with pain and fear? Or would you feel less burdened if you didn't have to wonder when his next violent outburst will occur?

4.   "If I leave him, he will kill me." If you don't leave, he may still kill you. In fact, some statistics show that many abusers become more violent when they feel rejected. This is why it is so important to seek help from counselors and those who will guide you through safe and effective ways to leave someone who is violent.

Women, stand up, respect, love and believe in yourselves. You are not a punching bag. Don't let anyone make you think that you are. Repeat to yourself, "I am somebody. I'm good. I can find love again." Keep saying it, because the more you say it the more you begin to believe it.

Has anyone ever called you a fat slob? Have you been told you were a piss-poor excuse for a woman? How did you feel? Did you feel like less of a person? Or did you say to yourself, "If I were a better person, it would not have happened?"

If you are constantly put down, talked about, or knocked down, you have experienced abuse. If he hits you once and you do not put a stop to it, he might do it again. If you or someone you know is in an abusive relationship, get help fast. Leave, but don't announce it. With the help of an experienced counselor you can strategically plan the safest way to leave.

The next time someone whispers, "I love you," after they have beaten you, remember, love does not hurt. Run! Run as fast as you can to the nearest shelter. If he hits you or puts you down by calling you hateful names, the next time he may kill you. Pay attention to the warning signs and make a decision to take care of yourself first.

Sumthin' T' Say

WHY DO I?

I know I could die,

When I don't take flight,

To get away from the person,

Who hit, slapped and kicked me.

You don't love me.

If you did, you wouldn't hurt me!

So why do I take this pain?

When it's you,

I no longer want to gain.

A LONG TIME AGO

I stopped loving you a long time ago;

The first time you knocked me to the floor.

You may think you are all that,

But this time, baby,

I'm not taking you back!

WHAT'S THE USE?

What's the use of being with you,

when you hit, insult and abuse me?

Why should I love you so,

when you've knocked me so many times

to the floor?

Why should I care so much,

when my heart hurts and feels like it's going to burst?

Every time I see your face,

it's filled with so much anger and hate.

If you want us to be together,

then we have to consult with the only one who matters.

Let's get counseling and pray together,

Get baptized, blessed and saved, and become better,

Because that's the only way,

I'm coming back to you.

You see, if you don't do these things,

I am truly through with you.

HEALTH

HEALTH MATTERS

While watching television or when reading magazines, the one topic that remains constant is that health matters. The concept of Body, Mind, Soul, & Spirit has become one of the most discussed topics, because it revolves around people and how they feel. When you feel good about yourself you will do things that are healthy, emotionally, mentally and spiritually, to retain that feeling.

Evidence suggests that people who do not take care of themselves, physically and emotionally, suffer from a variety of illnesses. Health problems such as depression, heart disease, obesity, diabetes and stress are just a few of the illnesses you may have when you neglect yourself. With all the problems parents are faced with, being unhealthy can only add to this frustration.

With today's hectic lifestyles, parents have less time and more frustration to handle on a daily basis. Problems, such as lack of reliable childcare, joblessness, housing and transportation, are major factors that can push an already stressed person over the edge. An important question should be, "What is a person to do?"

One thing you should do is look in the mirror and decide that you are important and valuable. Next, decide what areas of your life need attention. You must come to a conclusion that your body has served you well and now you must return the favor. You should not put yourself down negatively, but look at improvements as bonuses.

We must take care of ourselves because when we are healthy we can help others. When we feel well it becomes easier to support our children. What better reward for you and those you love than spending valuable time together?

Taking the time to nurture the body and mind are important steps to becoming healthy. Participating in exercise classes, stress and nutrition workshops, and having therapeutic massages are only

Sumthin' T' Say

a sampling of what we could do to feel better about ourselves.

If we are to continue carrying the torch for ourselves and our children we have to take care of ourselves. When we take care of our needs, it is much easier to help others. Remember that an ounce of self-gratification and positive attention toward yourself today may prevent a dose of medication tomorrow. Look at your, body, mind and spirit, and remember that beauty comes from inside and can be spread to others. Learn about your body, fulfill your mind, and watch your dreams and your spirit soar.

Rose Jackson-Beavers

APPLES, GOD AND PRAYER

They say have an apple a day,

But I say God is the way.

He will give you good health.

Just pray each day.

Be healthy.............

Be strong..............

You can't go wrong.

But still eat your apples

Everyday.

HEALTH

Health is your business.

Look at yourself.

Are you happy with your appearance?

Eat Right.

Exercise with all your might.

Take care of everything,

Right down to your eyesight.

When health is a goal,

And you want to achieve it,

Ask God through prayer.

He'll help you to receive it.

KNOWLEDGE

DOES KNOWLEDGE BREED POWER OR IS IT THE POTENTIAL TO HAVE POWER?

I have heard the saying, "Knowledge breeds power," so much throughout my life, yet I always related it more to economics than education. I felt that if you were knowledgeable you could obtain financial power. As I grew older, I realized this phrase could apply to my everyday thinking. I also see the relevance of being educated on the street verses education in the school system. Not that institutionalized education isn't important, because in many cases it's just as important as putting food in your mouth But depending on the situation, street education may be more advantageous when we are making decisions about family and life.

My mom educated me about sexuality, family and life. She would often say things like, "Little ladies do not do things like that," or "Don't sit with your legs like that." Most of the time I thought her prodding was meddlesome and would often say to myself, "Let me learn on my own," while thinking at the same time, Please leave me alone. But as I have grown older, I have become wiser.

When I gave birth to my daughter, I realized I would have to teach her many of the same things my mom had to teach me, including lessons about sexuality. My mother talked to my sisters and me, to let us know that we could always count on her. She wanted us to always feel comfortable discussing any issues with her. I have had to do the same with my daughter, because I would rather she ask me questions before listening to others who wouldn't have her best interest at heart.

One day she asked if she could spend the night with a former neighbor. In the years that I'd known that family, my daughter and I knew them to be friendly, kind and generous. They would often bring my child gifts and would come to visit her. When she was three years old, I noticed that the father would greet her with kisses on her lips. This made me feel very uncomfortable. At age five, I decided that it was the best time to begin educating my child about a variety of issues.

For instance, I explained to my daughter that it was improper for someone to kiss her on the lips. I said that was one of the ways germs spread from person to person. I further stated that it was best not to allow people to kiss her on lips until she was old enough to understand what kissing meant, and since we were on the subject, I decided to take the conversation further. I explained that if someone touched her in a place that made her uncomfortable to come and discuss it with me.

It was uncomfortable for me to witness a grown man kissing my child. I was concerned about the message it was giving her. Would an older man, who had previously given my daughter gifts, give her the wrong message by kissing her on the lips? The message being that it was okay to let men pay for her affection. While I was unsure of the message received from the man's actions, I was not about to leave the situation unaddressed.

I continued to explain to my child that she could not spend the night with everyone. I related this speech to incidents that occurred with me while visiting relatives and friends for sleepovers. One incident I clearly remember was when my cousin touched me inappropriately during a visit to Chicago. I remember when he pushed me in a corner and then prodded and touched me on my private parts.

I remember how uncomfortable I felt. Knowing it was wrong, I smacked my cousin as hard as I could and ran to my mom. Crying, I told her how he touched me on my private parts and she discussed the incident with his mom. To this day, I have never seen that cousin again. From that experience and others, I knew I could not send my daughter to spend the night with any and everybody, no matter who they were!

When I hear people say so freely that they will be sending their children to live with relatives for an entire summer, I shiver. Memories of how I felt when I was violated and the many horrible stories I'd heard from others who had experienced the same things would flood my mind. I could not imagine sending my young daughter off to stay with someone who may then be touching, prodding or intimidating her with sexual overtures. If a child's mind is too young to handle these kinds of situations, they could cause irreparable harm.

Oftentimes, I have also learned some of life's greatest lessons through the experiences of others. For instance, the other day I noticed that my twelve-year-old niece was carrying feminine products in expectation of her monthly cycle starting. When I asked her if she had already started her menstrual cycle she said she hadn't. She went on to explain how important it was to be prepared for the inevitable.

I knew that my sister had a bad experience with the start of her cycle. It started while she was at school and she felt horrible, particularly when someone told her she had a spot on the back of her pants. She was now trying to prevent her daughter from going through the same embarrassment. This experience is a prime example of how we can use the power of knowledge to determine a course of action.

Now that I think about it, I see how having previous information can help us make more informed choices. No, having knowledge is not power, but it is the potential for having power. For if you do not use your knowledge to better yourself or others, how can it really be powerful?

ANOTHER'S EXPERIENCE

We are blessed to have the sense,

To make decisions that won't make us whence

Our parents taught us what was right and wrong,

And when we strayed, we didn't portray,

the character our parents wanted us to display.

We used another's experience because we knew,

That they had knowledge about what we wanted to do.

They led the path and experienced the pain,

So that we would know how to use our brains.

Listen to what our elders say,

Their past experiences led the way.

They gave us their knowledge,

Hard knocks without college,

To prevent us from going through a bad experience.

If you love yourself heed their advice,

Next time a problem arises you won't think twice!

LOVE

MATTERS OF THE HEART

Years ago, many private citizens, political allies, democrats and republicans in the United States were immersed in the Clinton/ Lewinsky affair. Each individual had an opinion on whether the president of the United States should have been impeached because he told a lie to protect his wife and daughter from public ridicule. He denied allegations that he was having an affair. The question asked by many of his supporters was whether or not he was a good president, capable of leading the nation into the next millennium. Those who wanted him to fail put all their efforts into analyzing his personal life and questioning his leadership ability, when he could not in fact keep his vows to his wife.

However, in many African American homes, the focus was on the president's ability to do his job, not on his sex life. I have heard many situations where our black men have strayed, but with pain, strength and resiliency their wives have endured. While still being able to bounce back with prayer, spiritual and professional counseling, these women have been able to forgive and go on with full and happy lives.

Although, the president's sex life was a hot topic for all those concerned about who would lead our country, it also presented an open forum for many other issues. The first issue was whether or not president could be trusted. It is my opinion that, although adultery is morally wrong, as instructed in the Bible, everyone has done something we didn't want others to know about. In many cases, some of us have told little white lies to protect ourselves, as well as others who were involved in the situation. What did Mr. Clinton do in his personal life that granted us an open window into his bedroom?

The other concerned was whether or not Hillary should remain with a man who cheated on her.

To answer the first question, Mr. William Clinton did what other men do everyday, whether they are in public office, in the pulpit or in the choir. When a man is given the opportunity to experience a sexual encounter that doesn't involve love, how many men would not try it, especially if they could get away with it? Well, my friend, most men would do it. Why not? If a man can get a woman to participate in sexual acts prohibited by his wife, I'm sure he would try it. Isn't that why most men cheat? They want to experience a different kind of sex, a different feeling. At least that's what I've heard many men confess. Also, sex without love, is a fantasy. When a man can get a woman to have oral sex with him, without any expectations, what do you think he is going to do, especially when the woman doesn't expect him to reciprocate the act?

Regarding the second question, concerning whether Hillary should stay with a repeat offender, here's the way I see it. First, to each his own, because we all have our own values and beliefs. Think about it like this: Why should she leave? After all, she has been with the man for more than fifteen years. She knows he loves her. Otherwise, he would have left at some point in their marriage. Why should Hillary sacrifice her love; her rights to his life, his pension, his insurance policy; his daughter's right to have two parents and a huge monetary advance for a book on her relationship with the man? This woman loves her husband and knows his past and his pain. She knows his background, his family life and history. She understands his insecurities and in many cases, knows where he's been and where he's going. Why shouldn't she enjoy the ride, especially, if her husband has continued to love and cherish her body and heart without any decline in their sexual experiences?

I'm sure Hillary weighed the positive and negative consequences of letting her man go while making the decision to remain married. If you were married for twenty years to a man who has committed two known incidents of infidelity, but is an excellent provider, a loving and supportive father to his daughter, compassionate about his country, and considerate to you, would you leave him? No, you wouldn't. You would fight to get him back. You would not allow someone to just walk in and take your man. As a woman, you are going to hit the books, learn what he likes, ask him questions, and demonstrate that you love him. His love for his family will win every time, especially over a woman who will stoop so low that she would get down on her knees and service a man without a napkin. Whom would he choose, the other woman who probably has done this to other unsuspecting married men?

When a man steps out to have an affair, he wants to experience something different. He thinks the grass is greener on the other side. Once outside the "fence of emotion" he experiments, maybe tries it again, and then returns home. Many decide not to leave their wives and families because they have an emotional attachment to them. A man thinks he can have a sexual encounter and then return to regular family living. Actually, he might as well go home, because eventually he will become tired of sneaking around and being pressured by the other woman to leave his wife. If he really desires to leave his wife, the other woman certainly wouldn't have to pressure him to do it. He would do it on his own.

The question I posed to you was whether Hillary Clinton should leave her husband and I say with resounding passion, NO WAY. But may I add that since he tiptoed out on her, he should check her slippers at night to see where they lead. You never know whose bed they've been under.

THE HEART MATTERS

The heart matters, don't you see?

I fell in love with him, and him with me.

When others interfere in our affairs,

It only causes pain and problems, I declare.

It doesn't matter if one plays on the other,

As long as they remember, it's me they prefer.

So if a lover strays and wants to come back,

Just think, the poor child was on the wrong track.

It's okay to make one mistake,

because marriage, my friend, is simply, "Give and take."

WHEN YOU STRAY

When you stray and go away,

It hurts me so and makes me gray,

When you break my heart and my spirit in two,

It's worse than being in hell or caught in a catch-22.

When you decide you want to be honest,

And break-up with me to find another Queen Bee,

Just tell me openly,

You may be surprised to find out,

That a girl like me will totally agree.

MATTERS OF THE HEART

No matter what the problem may be, infidelity or a lack of communication,

When you made the decision to marry, God blessed this creation.

When someone is unhappy because their spouse did wrong,

It won't change a thing because your marriage is lifelong.

You must work out your problems,

And do your best to solve them.

Even though the pain you feel may take some time to heal,

Remember the way you felt when your eyes first met,

Then all the other stuff won't cause you to fret.

The heart matters and that is a fact.

When you married each other, you made a solid pact.

Next time there's a problem, no need to overreact!

KOOL BREEZE

As I sit here thinking about my life and wondering how I ended up like this, I sigh. Could life be this miserable for others or am I being singled out? If I am, by who and why?

I often reflect on my life and the lives of others. Who are we and why are we here? Are we here to be servants and please others, or to seek pleasure from men whom we seem to need? If we are not here to please the male species, then why do we suffer so much pain from rejection when they no longer need us?

Sitting on the porch, I can feel a soft, kool breeze gently blow on my face. It feels nice and airy out here and I feel safe. I think about my family life and the friends I have met along the way. I think about my future and what I need to do to be happy for me and only me.

It seems as if women have to suffer a lot of pain to find out how strong we really are. If we have to suffer so much adversity, so much hopelessness, then it would seem as if we could choose our own way of suffering. We wouldn't leave it in the hands of a man who wants us to feel like we are less than others.

Men have an uncanny way of telling us what they feel. Once you have been with one of them long enough, they will tell you anything. They don't care how it hurts you. By instilling low self-esteem in us, their demanding, hot tempers tell us that we are no good, that we are bitches and unfit women. Why do we take this? Do we take the putdowns because of our own low expectations about who we are or what we want out of our lives?

As women we are too proud to be lonely, too proud to feel defeated, because we can't let go when we need to. So we hang onto pain because we think it is better than suffering alone. We hang onto men who mean us no good because we feel it is better than searching for someone better; because we are comfortable with what we already have.

Sumthin' T' Say

Letting the kool breeze whip across my face, I can feel the breeze becoming stronger. The stronger the breeze, the better it feels. Kool Breeze. A man. Kool breeze, a wind so soft, I can feel it touch my nerves and tingle my bones. Where does the breeze come from and how long will it last? Will it linger and come back tomorrow to make me feel this way? Or will the kool breeze fade, as the men in our lives do, when they decide to leave us for what they say is a better place?

Women must become strong and develop a positive attitude about themselves. We must continue to handle problems and pain as we have so many times in the past, and realize that life has more to offer us than a man! Knowing this will help us handle the pain men inflict upon us. In spite of the problems, we must and will persevere. To progress we must continue to survive, to conquer and deal with our fate, and allow the kool breeze to gently whip across our faces. A man? No, the gentle breeze of the wind!

KOOL BREEZE

Kool Breeze, everyone should know,

Is a Kool Cat,

With a Big Bad show.

See him walk with a dip,

About to break his left hip,

Looking for a vulnerable woman,

To kiss her lonely lips.

See that hat,

He wears cocked to one side.

Look at that man,

so full of it and he's jive.

Don't let that man,

Sweep you off your feet.

He just wants you as his next treat.

Kool Breeze,

A man, a Bad Cat,

Kick his butt to the wind,

Or he'll just keep coming back.

TOUCHING ME

Touch me, No not there!
Put your hands through my hair.
Love me, teach me,
Pull out a chair.
Show me you love me,
Show me you care.
Guide me, show me,
Give me the things,
That will teach me to,
Fulfill all my dreams.
Wake me, shake me,
Give me the strength,
To love you as long as the day's length.
Lead me, tell me all about you,
So I will know you,
Through and through.
When all these things are done to me,
I can become all that,
I want to be!

THINKING OF YOU

Tossing and turning, thinking of you.

Wanting and needing you like a fool.

You broke my heart, you took my faith,

When you ran away.

How could you say you loved me when,

You knew your love didn't come from within?

How could you hurt me and give me so much pain,

When I'm the one you wanted to gain?

To touch me, to kiss me,

To screw out my brains, then turn right around,

And cause me so much pain.

I trusted you, I believed in you.

I wanted to be all those things a woman to you should be.

You stepped on me, you hated me,

When you're the one who first loved me!

WHERE ARE YOU?

Where are you when you're not with me?

Where are you and who do you see?

If it's not me,

Then where can you be?

In a ship on the sea?

Or on a beach being unreachable for me.

I need a man I can count on.

I need a man I can trust.

No, I don't want to be alone,

But that's how it is when you're running around.

Are you considering me,

When you can't see the pain and problems you're causing me?

If you're not with me I'm gonna have to let you be.

If you don't want me just tell me,

So I can leave and start to believe,

In me, myself and, yes, the Lord!

Where are you,

When you're not with me?

Is this how it's going to be?

LONG DISTANCE LOVE

I miss seeing your kind face.

I hate that you're not in our special place.

It pained me when you went away.

I'm not able to face another day.

You are my blessing, my dream, my life.

I sometimes wish I was your wife.

Touch my hand, touch my face.

Slow and without haste,

Yeah, I got a love for you,

That just won't wait.

YOU WENT AWAY

Feeling so sad, being without you,

Feeling so bad, losing you,

Why did you leave me,

When you said I was the best

You ever had?

Why did you go when you said,

You loved me so?

Why did you ever walk out the door?

I don't understand.

When you said you were my man,

Then walked out on me without giving me a chance,

To understand.

I've got to come up with a plan,

To win you back, to get your love.

You walked out on me without even a word.

The pain so great I cannot say,

Why you ever had to go away!

WOMEN'S ISSUES

WOMEN ON THE MOVE

Society's perceptions about women as barefoot, pregnant homemakers went out in the late '70s and early '80s, along with polyester leisure suits and eight-track tapes. The notion that women are incapable of handling business, finances and community affairs is slowly becoming a myth that we as women have fought hard to change. The women of today no longer just worry about how to get a man through his stomach by, cooking his favorite meal or baking a tasty pie. We are capable of running large corporations and mandating new laws.

We as women are making major decisions that affect our families as well as our country. Women have sought out the same respect and restitution for our invaluable and informative advice about a variety of topics and situations. Yet, many times we are not recognized or given the credit we deserve. As our courage and passion grows, we continue to move forward and support many other important projects with the same directness, intuitiveness and inspiration. Women are encouraging others to accomplish their goals.

In the '90s and through the millennium we have seen women who designed and built airplanes, developed computer software, and headed cities and states as political leaders, as well as corporations and educational institutions. Women have built bridges and houses, entered into outer space, ran races, jumped hurdles, and nurtured, raised and loved our families and friends, as we continued to push forward to a new century. These are only small samplings of our capabilities and of what is yet to come. Not only are women making a name for themselves throughout the country, but many are coming back to their communities and helping others achieve their personal goals.

Take Jackie Joiner-Kersee for example. A known sports figure in track & field, she has achieved numerous personal goals. But throughout her career she continued to speak positively about her community. She even spoke highly and often of her childhood coach, giving him national acknowledgment, and she continued to utilize him as her mentor and coach often throughout her career. Now she is reaching back into her community to build a state of the art recreational and sports center, so the kids in her community can be afforded many of the same opportunities to develop their skills that she had.

Women are on the move as they continue to rise to the top and soar to the highest peaks. Women are more determined now than ever to make their dreams come true. As these women continue to move mountains, let's continue to follow their lead and help all our brothers and sisters fulfill their own dreams. Let's do what these women have done by pushing, encouraging and inspiring others to accomplish goals. You never know, you could be introducing another Jackie to the world.

Rose Jackson-Beavers

WOMEN ON THE MOVE

Women on the move to conquer the world,

From pigtails, braids and beautiful curls,

Accomplishments, success and achieving goals,

We are a heck of a group, with great self-control.

If we want to sing, dance, write or teach,

We can do anything within or out of our reach.

Astronaut, computer technician, civil engineer, or preacher,

So many occupations you can't reach without a teacher.

The women of today, as from the past,

Will grow stronger and stronger and we will continue to last.

Now that, my friend, is our future forecast.

SUCCESS

Curls, braids, or your hair pressed,

Blouses, skirts, pants or a dress,

Women today strive for the best.

If a raise is what they want, or to meet a goal or pass any test,

Women are willing to work hard and do their best,

Even when they have to go through a lot of stress.

When the goal is obtained, they are not willing to rest,

Until they help another sister become a success.

MOTHERS

A MOTHER'S LOVE

Mother told me one day,

That I needed to learn and,

Lead the way.

To show the youth of the day,

A better way to work and play.

Show them Love,

She would say.

This way they will know the way.

Teach them and guide them.

Do as I did.

Make them want to be,

An example for others to follow.

Mother said.

Mother did.

Mother loved us, Oh yes she did.

THOUGHTS FROM PARENTS

Tomorrow is the first day,

Without your parents in your way.

Along the road you learned the things,

That would help you always.

We'll miss you,

But we'll always remember those themes,

That helped you dream,

When you finally put away all your schemes.

Live your life to the fullest.

Love your children from the heart.

Remember that we are always with you.

Always, even from the start.

Rose Jackson-Beavers

MOTHER

My mother loved us so,

And she gave and gave,

Until she could give no mo!

MAMA

I love you more than you could know.

You raised me well and then said, "go."

You left me there all by myself,

As if I would sit there as neatly as books on a shelf.

But I took the knowledge you instilled in my soul,

Pulled my shoulders back and held my head high,

As I walked as tall and straight as a totem pole.

With a college degree in my hand,

Your blessings and words of encouragement,

Playing in my head like drums in a band,

Helped me quickly take a powerful stand.

Being on my own and having to do,

All those things you made me redo,

Made me the person I am today.

Successful, respectful and your protégé,

Because you're the best mama in the whole USA.

HAVING YOU

I'm so glad I have you to go to for advice.

How else would I learn to be a better wife?

Being able to discuss my problems,

Sure helped me to resolve them.

This makes me feel great,

Because having you for a mother,

Only makes me first rate!

Thank you for supporting me,

Through high school, college and then,

For understanding and loving me when,

I didn't pay attention to anything,

Including you, telling me to have positive friends.

Your patience, guidance and tolerance,

Helped me through so many days and nights of problems.

You supported me when I needed you the most,

With your help I will continue to be a good wife and that you can toast!

DRUGS

DRUGS

Drugs are not the way,

To make you feel better on any day.

Using illegal drugs won't dull the pain.

There is nothing that you will gain.

Pain, misery, thievery too,

That's all drugs have to offer you.

I WON'T DO DRUGS

Don't look my way,

You should say.

I won't do drugs any day!

Don't try to sell them to me,

and my friends.

We don't need them,

To make us feel in.

IN THE BACK ROOM

Someone is doing drugs in the smoke-filled back room,

Living their life day to day in total gloom and doom.

Didn't finish school, thought they were too cool,

When all they did was prove they are a plumb fool.

Now they spend their time sleeping during the day,

Like a vampire at night, searching to get high,

Without a dime to give a drug dealer for pay.

So they steal, rob and kill,

To continue to take the disgraceful drug pill.

Too cracked out to seek help and assistance,

When all you need is prayer to quit and have a fighting chance,

With a desire to change and become clean,

The Lord our God will certainly intervene,

With your desire and His will,

no more drugs or caffeine,

because now your body and blood are squeaky clean.

No more drugging in a smoke-filled back room,

all that's left is a life filled with peace and serene.

MARRIAGE

THE MOST DIFFICULT CHALLENGE

Marriage is the most difficult challenge I have ever faced. It is more difficult than having a baby, because you get over the pain of giving birth. It is more difficult than raising a child, because you are the adult and you can take charge. It is more difficult than working for a terrible boss, because you can quit and get another job. It is more difficult than going through college, because you can study and graduate, or quit and go home. It is more difficult than losing weight, because you can either accept yourself for who you are, diet and lose the weight, or have surgery. It is more difficult than learning to walk, because you can always just crawl. Marriage is the most difficult to handle because there are two people with different dreams, hopes and desires to consider. In marriages you have to bring two different ideas or opinions together and become a team. Your thought process changes from "me" to "us" and that in itself is very difficult.

A successful marriage takes combining your dreams, finances, families, and your goals into ones that will benefit two thriving and sometimes selfish people. If marriages are to survive, you need money to take you through struggles and times of hunger. You also need vision to dream of a future together. And most importantly, you need prayer and a relationship with God to smooth out the bumps.

In my opinion, having a relationship with God is the single most important ingredient in staying married. Without these four things and your love for each other, your marriage could end up in serious trouble.

Today, with the high cost of living and the competition for success, you desperately need to have your finances in order. Many people spend more money than they actually have, to impress others. They are really perpetrating a fraud by showing off their so-called assets, clothes, diamonds and their luxury cars, when they struggle to pay their monthly bills. If the husband is the main bread winner and your spending is in direct opposition to what he expects, this causes frustration and anger. There are many people who will spend beyond their means simply to keep up with the "Jones'."

Yet, if you think about it, how can you keep up with someone when you don't know the amount of money that person has? Purchasing the latest car, furniture and home may be as simple as making a call, if you have the money. But for someone who is without the necessary finances, overspending is easy to do.

In many marriages, when one spouse disrespects the other by constantly spending, the result can be a fruitless trip to divorce court. Most polls regarding divorce list money as the number one reason. This would leave one to believe that in order to have a successful relationship you need to have your finances in order. The old saying, "Money is the root of all evil," is becoming more of a reality to me.

If there is too little money, you're constantly arguing about what bills need to be paid or who will pay the bills.

These arguments lead to fights and harsh words about each other. Your days as a couple are about to end because you're tired of scraping together money to survive and you feel no respect for your other half because of the negative names they've called you. After so many arguments, your love begins to grow cold and you begin to work against each other. You can't forget the names you were called just because you spent money that you made. When there is too much struggling, there is no room for growth and this could quickly lead you to divorce court.

When there is too much money, you splurge, spend and have a good time. But the problem with constant spending is that you never get a chance to save anything. For the saver who looks to the future to enjoy his or her retirement years without financial worries, this could be a serious breach of trust and respect. The spender tries to enjoy life today, because he or she doesn't know if they will even be here tomorrow. This person may need immediate gratification. This attitude may infuriate the saver, who believes that you should always have an abundance of money for a rainy day. When there is a difference in attitudes and you don't have the same goals as a twosome, you will eventually become a one some.

In most marriages, you struggle to attain money and you struggle to retain it. If there are too many arguments you become delusional, and you feel that there has to be someone better out there who would love and respect you and who could take care of your financial needs. So you spend your days dreaming, visualizing and wishing for passionate love with a prince who will take you away from your penny-pinching spouse.

When you are unhappy in a marriage, you spend time pouting and living in a fantasy world, rather than dealing with the problems at hand. Then one day you come to the realization that the two perfect people who were married don't exist anymore. What does exist are two people with a lot of struggles and pain who have to learn to work together while learning to accept each other's differences, something neither of you may be willing to do at this time in your marriage.

To have a successful marriage, your love for each other must outweigh your troubles and you must have prayer and a close relationship with God. You must be able to talk openly to your spouse and listen to the concerns that are presented. To succeed in love, you must be willing to sacrifice some of your dreams and help your spouse seek his own, as well. You must trust that the two of you will make decisions that are in the best interest of the family. If that means deciding on a new budget that the two of you can live with, go for it.

You may have to set aside a certain amount of money to put away for the future and receive an allowance. You must work hard to have common goals that are shared by both of you, because marriage is such a difficult challenge and it will take hard work, perseverance and sacrifice to make your love last. As a married couple, you must do what it takes to stay married. After all, once you enter a marriage blessed by God, there is no divorce.

THE MOST DIFFICULT CHALLENGE

Love is the most difficult challenge for two people to sustain,

Letting go of the single life and all of its chains,

To live life as a couple, with friends who will remain.

With hopes that no problems will hinder or connive,

The marriage or the lovers as they continue to strive,

To share their life, dreams and goals,

As they become not one person, but a whole.

The most difficult challenge was when,

The man carried his woman over the threshold,

As he promised her he would continue to have self-control,

To leave other women behind,

And to make her his special one of a kind.

When the woman agreed to make him her man,

She didn't do it with a ball and chain,

But with love in her heart,

She agreed to make him a part,

Of her life forever and she would never depart.

So the most difficult challenge shouldn't be a problem,

Remember your vows and do your best to resolve them.

WILL THE REAL WOMEN PLEASE STAND UP?

A real woman, as defined by Jackson-Beavers, is a female who respects herself, others and her relationships. She represents her family well by making trustworthy decisions that are rational and well thought out. She does not disrespect others and their properties.

A real woman will do whatever it takes to avoid breaking up someone else's home by having an affair with another woman's husband or partner. A real woman may date a man whom she thinks is single, based on what he has said to her, but the minute she discovers that he is married or otherwise involved, she will choose never to see him again.

I realize there are many women who believe that if they get involved with a married man and fall in love, there is nothing they can do to alter the situation. In their opinion, it is too late to leave, because they love him and their heart is involved. If you happen to find yourself in this situation, the best thing to do is think about your own heart. How would you feel if it were your husband that another woman was seeing and was in love with? What would you do? After carefully considering your feelings, think about the man's wife and family. A considerate and compassionate person would not only think of their own feelings, but would also look at how their actions affect their fellow man. Once you look at the situation in this respect, you can't help but stop the negative and self-defeating behavior of seeing or dating a married man.

A question to ponder: If a women feels good about herself, would she allow someone to make her a second fiddle? Most women don't take the time to really look in the mirror and give themselves positive affirmations, saying things like, "I am important" or "I am beautiful." If we believed we were beautiful and important, it would be difficult for someone to pull the wool over our eyes, especially a married man with bad intentions. When we feel depressed and lonely, it makes it easy for someone who is out looking for a good time to target poor souls like us.

They have already figured out that you're so desperately seeking companionship that you would be willing to share your man.

If women continue to downplay their own happiness and deny their feelings of wanting a relationship of their own, they will always be unhappy without a man. This will lead them to feel like they are second-rate and will always receive others' leftovers. So they spend their lives looking for Mr. Right by constantly dating Mr. Wrong.

It is easy for some woman to accept a man who is already taken, because it makes the pain of not having someone of their own less difficult to handle. Women can always use the excuse that they are in love with someone, so they won't have to admit that they don't have a man of their own. Dealing with the whys may cause a woman to analyze why she can't find someone who is not already taken to love. Is it something the woman lacks, such as low self-esteem? Or maybe they have the, "I think I'm better than any man syndrome"?

Women should exhibit the same traits in themselves that they want from a man. When they do this, it will be harder for a married man, out looking for a one-night stand or two, to deceive the encouraging woman. If women want to stop hurting, why won't they take more interest in looking into these men's backgrounds?

For instance, when a person wants to purchase a car, they do everything to find the best bargain. They comparison shop, do surveys, seek advice from family and friends about the car's performance or any other information that would help them make the best decision. Another example of checking out something before we get involved is seeking information for a new job. Before we accept a new position, we check the libraries for information on the company, talk to current and past employees, and will even go so far (at least some of us) as to check the Brad & Dunstreet book to assure it is a reputable company.

Yet, when it comes to choosing a man, we take less time looking into his background than it takes to say yes to the question, "Will you go out with me?" Others will simply take any man who seems available or who looks the part just to be with a man. All the man has to say is, "Want to go out?", and the woman thinks, "He's handsome, got a nice car, a good job and money. I'll take him."

Some women take more pride in searching for a house, a job or a new pair of shoes than they take in selecting a man to spend their time with. What about checking out the man, is he attached by marriage or does he have a family? Who is his family? Does he love his mother and treat her with respect? Does he have a police record or has he been in prison? Is he promiscuous? Drug and disease free? Does he go to church? If so, which one? Does he have a job? These are the kinds of questions one should consider before deciding on dating a person.

I have heard some women make statements about why they are dating married men. For example, some do it to keep from being lonely. Others may not want a man around them twenty-four hours a day, seven days a week. But I ask you this question: Would you rather be lonely or forgotten on holidays? Whom does the man share the important holidays of the year with, you or his family? Or is he the kind of man who sneaks out around nine to see you on Christmas or Thanksgiving Day and rushes back home to be with his family. Are you lonely then? When do you see the married man, once or twice a week for about two or three hours? I'm sure the man is busting his butt home before his wife misses the time he's gone. So what are you really getting, a man who can't give you the time of day?

Now, I know women want to be with a special man, but rather than believing the myth that most black men are on drugs, homosexual, dead or in jail, what about looking at the blue collar worker, or the maintenance man, or the bus driver, who makes an honest living? They are all equally hard working and respectful, and deserve a good woman. What about the man who has a heart filled with love, ready and waiting to share it with a special lady who believes in him?

There are many available black men who don't have a college education, but who have street sense, and who will work hard at providing for their loved ones. He may be a man who couldn't go to college because of circumstances. Perhaps he was the oldest child and had to care for sick parents and that's why he didn't go to college. Look at the reason he didn't pursue education, rather than the fact that he doesn't have one before you to say, "I'm not interested." A man who gave away opportunities to care for his sick parents is unselfish and loving and to me, a far better catch than one who thinks he's all that and wouldn't lift a finger to help someone in need.

As women, we have to look at his character rather than his salary, because where he may fall short, we can make it up with our skills. When choosing a spouse or mate, look at whether he respects you and his family. Is he considerate of you and others? Is he kind? Does he get along well with children? Isn't a man of good character one we should seek? Ladies, please take the same care and time you spend choosing material things to also select your lifelong mate. After all, this is the man you want to have babies with and live the rest of your life with.

If I could leave women with a word of advice, it would be to do background checks and investigate potential love interests. If he is married and is bold enough to tell his wife he loves her, and then leave home to meet you and tell you the same, he is worse than a criminal and nothing more than a thief. He specializes in breaking hearts and leaving women afraid of hurting and more reluctant to fall in love again.

So my friend, I ask you: Is it better to have half of a man than a whole one? Or half a heart, because that is how you will feel every time he leaves you to go back to his wife? Remember that what goes around comes around and when it comes back to you, the hurt is three times more painful because your suffering will be accompanied by guilt and flashbacks of what you did. My question to you, my sister, is, "Are you a real woman or a woman playing with real women's toys?"

Think about it and while you're doing that, will the real women please stand up?

MAN BLUES

Sitting here so all alone,

Without a man to call my own,

Watching the time fly by,

It makes me wonder, "Why?"

I have no man at my side,

Someone my mother can call her son.

Or maybe a man who would call and just say, "hi!"

Then I won't have to hear the word, "goodbye."

I have man blues,

No gold, gray or other colors in the sky,

Man blues and I don't know why!

Have you ever had man blues?

If you haven't, you would really miss those dudes.

Man blues, boy, dude or guy,

It doesn't matter what you call them,

I just know I want a piece of that pie.

HOW CAN I?

How can I go wrong,

With you on my side?

How can I not love you,

When all you do is try,

To please me with your smiles,

While telling everyone you love me

Just by the twinkling of your eyes?

ETHNICITY

SHADES OF COLORS

Several years ago, while watching a nightly news show, I saw a study about African-American children and why they have low self-esteem regarding the color of their skin. Comparisons of two dolls, an African-American doll and a Caucasian doll, were made to determine which doll was the most beautiful. All of the children interviewed were preschool students, who each selected the Caucasian doll as the most beautiful doll of the two.

The results showed that, as early as preschool, children are being taught that the color of their skin determines whether or not they are considered beautiful.

During the segment, both dolls, which were dressed identically, were held up for each child to see and then the interviewer asked each child to identify the most beautiful of the two dolls. Specifically, the interviewer asked, "Which is the most beautiful?" Every black child in the room selected the Caucasian doll. The interviewer then asked the children: "Why did you pick the white doll, when they have on the same clothes?" Several of the children replied that the black doll was dirty because her skin was black. Who is teaching our African-American children that, because they have dark skin, they are dirty, unclean, or unattractive?

This is a question we must begin to evaluate and determine a course of action to eliminate negative feelings about ourselves. Although, that study was done with children, the results would probably be the same if it were done with African-American men as the subjects. Otherwise, how else could it be explained that many African-American men prefer women outside of their own race for dating and marriage?

African-American women are the most beautiful, sophisticated and strongest women in the world. Although many negative situations might permeate their daily lives, they have continued to move forward through hurt and pride to persevere. What other race would be able to survive so much pain and misery, now and from the past, and continue to wear a smile to mask their situation?

There are none. Who could take being put down and called negative names because of the color of their skin, then turn around and lie still while the master grunts and humps on their tired and bruised bodies? Yes, we are indeed a beautiful group of people who have withstood so much rejection and shame, and we continue to endure.

Lately, there has been a lot of emphasis on the skin color of African-American women. One of the reasons this has become a major focus has to do with the increase in interracial relationships and marriages. Many black women are at a loss as to why so many of their brothers are veering to the other side. The belief is held by many that African-American brothers are color-struck. They believe white is right and that being with a white woman is a sign to others that they are successful. Some feel being seen with a woman of another race makes them a man who can finally hold his head high, because he has done the one thing that was forbidden for him to do in his struggle to be an accomplished black man.

What is wrong with this picture? It implies that African-American women are not as desirable or respected as other races.

We are a race of people who come in many different shades, shapes and sizes. If a man is not interested in a woman of a darker complexion, he can have his choice of any of the colors of the rainbow. For the man who prefers the brighter side of things, his choices can range from cappuccino, caramel, and tawny, to cinnamon, taupe and copper tones.

For the man who believes the saying, "The blacker the berry, the sweeter the juice," he has his choice of cocoa brown, maple brown, milk chocolate, and mahogany. So if the beautiful and sexy African-American man is looking for someone who can meet more than one area of his desires, look to the black woman.

It doesn't matter whom you love, but the problem arises when some African-American men actually seek out women of other races, and this perplexes me for many reasons. Mainly because Caucasian women always seek ways to look like us. They spend countless dollars trying to change their skin color, which seems to be the very thing many of our men prefer. They lie on the beach for hours so their skin tone will darken like ours, or they pay by the hour to lie on a tanning bed. Another trend has been for Caucasian women to take fat from some other part of their bodies and inject it into their lips. This makes their lips thicker and fuller. Ironically, these are seemingly the same lips successful black men run from. But in dating Caucasian women he might find himself right back where he started.

The sad part of this message is, for those who date outside their race, many of our black men are not looking for what is inside of their women, like heart, emotions, etc. They seem to be looking at skin color alone. It is destructive for a successful black man to turn his back on his race because he feels we are not good enough. It's enough that we have to face our own struggles, but when we also have to be rejected and put down by black men, it makes the pain greater. It further causes women to beat themselves up, and to develop a lower level of security and poor self-esteem.

Sadly, it seems unless you are a rich sports figure that if a black man finds a woman of another race, she is usually one who is having a hard time finding love within her own race, because she is deemed not as attractive or does not have what it takes to be acceptable among other Caucasians. The black man who buys into the concept that white is better will knock his own mother down to get to this woman, because, as long as she is white, he is happy.

My advice to black men is, if you want real love; someone who knows the pain you've experienced; someone who knows your struggles because they have shared the same; someone who knows how it feels to be put down because of the color of their skin; someone who has lost jobs and other opportunities, because it was assumed that they were incapable of achieving, look to the beautiful African-American woman. She has the history to support facts and she will stick with you or to you when the going gets tough. Believe me when I say she will not revert back to the mentality of slavery and past times, by calling you every name in the book when she becomes angry.

When a black sister can love a black man with freedom to express herself and without being compared to white women, not only will Black men have the strength to overcome adversities, but, because they have someone who understands their pain, they will also have a powerful motivator.

A black woman will let her man know it is unacceptable to give up, that she expects him to get up and do what she knows he can do to make his life more satisfying. A black woman will make her black man feel more complete, because she knows where he is going or could go and because she knows where he has been.

Shades of color mean more than the obvious color of one's skin. It means acceptance, understanding and the ability to know who you are, without having to look through someone else's eyes. Now don't get me wrong, I am not prejudiced. If you happen to fall in love with someone outside of your race, let love happen! But choosing to love someone because of their race is a travesty, because your intentions are not honorable. You will be entering into a relationship doomed to fail, based on lies, the first of which being the one you told yourself.

If you are a brother who has dated or married someone of another race because you genuinely love your lady, that's absolutely great. However, for the brother who searched for the "perfect" white woman to make him feel better about himself, shame on you! You haven't done anything to be proud of. Instead, you have set yourself and your family up for a lifetime of identity problems, and, my brother, it takes a love strong and pure to grasp the problems of integrating into a society that already doesn't believe in you. Remember that love deals strictly with the heart, not the shade of skin color.

SHADES OF COLOR

Shades of color like red, white and blue,

Black just doesn't seem a part of this color hue.

Men who can't deal with themselves when they look in the mirror,

Are a pitiful disappointment and this can't be any clearer.

If they don't understand their responsibility to their race,

We need to let them go and let them have their space.

As a member of the African-American race,

We've had so many difficult problems to face,

It hurts us badly when we put down our own race,

It's just as bad as being hit hard in the head with a vase.

If we can't accept ourselves for the color of our skin,

It's a shame and a pity and we'll never win.

How can we ever improve our lives,

When some black men will never make us their wives?

How can we ever teach our children to have positive self-esteem,

When their fathers believe white is supreme?

When we can love ourselves,

Everybody else will stop putting our ideas on the shelves.

SPIRITUALITY

CHRISTIAN

I'm a Christian.

I'm a Christian.

Can't you see?

God won't let anyone,

Mess with me.

If I read my Bible,

And pray everyday,

God said He'd protect me,

From day to day.

If someone tells you to do something wrong,

Run, don't walk, until you get away.

THE WORLD

The world is a great big place,

So big you can't cover it, not even in a race.

Be humble, prayerful and appreciative,

And don't do anything negative or in bad taste.

One day the Lord will return and take us to a place so beautiful,

Big, powerful and great.

It's there for each of us, if we have faith.

Be good and faithful and let's run this race.

We can win it,

If we keep our mind in good taste,

And our feet in a safe, blessed place.

IN YOUR TIME OF SORROW

As you go through the days and nights,

Remember God will make everything all right.

Trust in him, he'll be there for you.

He will bring you comfort both day and night.

Remember, you are a diamond,

Full of light, shining brightly like sun during the night.

You lost someone special in your life.

Go ahead, grieve, girl, it's all right.

God promised us He'd make our burdens light.

He loves us with all his might.

That's why I know you'll be all right.

Written for Rose Mary Tally

Homage to her son, John Tally

LIKE YOU, JESUS

Like you, Jesus, I strive to be,

Loving, faithful and compassionate, you see.

Help me to always love others, in my efforts to be like you.

Teach me to pray so I'll know what to say and do.

Walk with me through the night and protect me, too.

Help me encourage others, as they, too, try to be like you.

When I'm feeling sad and blue and I don't know what to do,

Show me, lead me and push me, if you have to.

Lord, remember me,

Cause I'm the girl who wants to be just like YOU!

BELIEVE

I can't believe what God has done.

He will help you win every race you run.

Trust in Him, He'll be there for you.

Believe in prayer, that's what He gave to you.

He'll answer your prayers, if you believe in Him, too.

Loving God is the least you can do,

Because caring for you is what He said He would do.

Isn't God trying to tell us something,

So we will know what to do?

I betcha' if you read the book of Revelations,

you'd know that too!

GOD IS GOOD

God is so good and compassionate, too.

If you only believe in Him,

You'll know that, too.

He is so merciful and will be there,

When you are blue.

To be with Him,

You must know what to do.

Be kind to others and respectful, too,

Keep the commandments, like He told us to do,

Pray and ask Him to forgive you for your sins.

Do that for Him and you'll see Him again.

God is good.

Aren't you glad,

You know him, too?

Rose Jackson-Beavers

DO YOU BELIEVE IN GOD?

Do you really believe in God?

Or do you think you do?

Do you study His word,

The Bible, all the way through?

Do you believe, He'll save you,

Like He promises to do?

To take you to heaven to live with Him,

His angels and other Christians, too.

Or do you go through the motions,

Pretending, faking and acting like you do?

Jesus knows our hearts and souls,

So stop faking, you're only fooling you.

Do you believe in God?

If so, why don't you start,

 Walking, talking and acting like you do?

HOLY SPIRIT

Quiet......
Can you hear the Holy Spirit?
Listen.......
So softly and tenderly,
A voice....
In the distance, yet so sweet.
It offers you a choice,
Between doing what's right and what's wrong,
Between using drugs or being really strong.
Listen........
To the Holy Spirit,
If it is Jesus you want to meet,
Ask Him for guidance and one day,
It's He that you will see!

Rose Jackson-Beavers

WITH MY HEAD TOWARD THE SKY

Walking with my head toward the sky,

Makes me feel like I'm on a natural high.

Thanking God for all my things,

And for allowing me to achieve all my dreams.

The sky so blue,

So calming too,

With streaks of all colors,

In the hue.

Makes me appreciate God even more,

For being my Lord and my Savior, too.

GOD DID IT

It's snowing, so white and fluffy,

It's time to go outside,

 with your sleds and other fun stuff.

For me, it's a time to reflect on life,

To see the beauty from God, the Almighty,

To know he made the spring, summer, fall and winter.

Thinking about this makes me feel hot and happy in midwinter.

The things God has done are so great and grand.

It lets me know that God had a plan.

He made the sun, stars, the moon and land,

So that one day when He comes back,

We'll all see the rest of His master plan.

MISPLACED TRUST

Do you have misplaced trust?

Think about this, because if you do,

It can make your poor heart rust.

Having misplaced trust and not believing,

What God can do,

Can make a strong, soft heart,

Turn cold and blue,

 And ultimately your heart will fall apart.

Do you have misplaced trust?

Because if you don't have someone to believe in today,

It's just as bad as losing your voice and having nothing to say!

With misplaced trust,

You're allowing your poor heart to rust,

And that, my friend, is worse than eating sawdust!

SOMETHING GOOD

Something good is going to happen to you,

No matter what you say or what you do.

If you are kind, gentle and nice,

Others will care for you,

Without thinking twice,

To treat you right,

With all their might.

To respect and appreciate you,

Without you being in their eyesight.

Treat others wrong,

And it won't be long,

To find that you are so very alone.

something good is going to happen to you,

It's all about what you say and what you do!

Rose Jackson-Beavers

IS THE DEVIL IN YOU?

Is the devil in you?

Think of all the things you do.

Is the devil in you?

Think about this issue all the way through.

Is the devil in you?

If so, you know what to do.

Ask God to help you,

And you have to help yourself, too!

The Lord said, "If you seek the kingdom first,"

He will certainly fulfill your thirst.

If the devil is in you?

Give it to the Lord,

And he will bless you and your heart he'll renew.

IT IS NOT YOURS

This battle is not yours,

It is the Lord's.

Problems, pain and discouragement,

Will always be a part of your life.

But God said to come to him,

He'll make everything all right.

You know this battle isn't yours,

It is the Lord's.

Prayer, fasting and reading his word,

Will bring joy to your soul,

And spirit to your heart,

All the way down,

From your head to your toes.

No, this battle is not yours,

Just give it to the Lord.

WHEN I

When I close my eyes and dream,

I see so many beautiful things.

The sky, clouds, the moon and sun,

All this lets me know there is a great one.

When I close my eyes and meditate,

I can't help but think,

About those who hate and those who love and care.

It makes me feel that God is really there!

When I close my eyes and think,

I feel like I really am in synch,

With my spouse, my child, my parents and my friends,

It makes me feel the spirit within.

When I close my eyes and feel,

I know that God is really real,

To me, to you, and all the world,

And that is why,

I strive hard to be a perfect girl.

BLACK PRIDE

MARTIN LUTHER KING, JR.

He was a great man,

Whom God gave a plan.

He said, help my people.

Give them a hand.

Use your voice,

So that my people will have a choice,

To do the things,

That they want to do.

Talk and be heard,

All across this land,

Tell them what they are doing,

To hold back black peoples' hand.

Tell them that I don't want them,

To act like that!

"Martin," God said, "when you are done,

I'll bring you home to me, my dear son."

WHY DO OTHERS PUT ME DOWN?

I can't understand why others put me down,

A person with black skin,

They don't want me around.

When I see things that my race has done,

It's a wonder why they try to gun us down.

For instance, who made the mop,

Because they were tired of being on their knees,

Cleaning the master's floor,

While bruising their self-esteem?

Who made the stem in the light bulb,

Because they were tired of living off the sun?

Who made the plasma in blood,

So our men could live,

And continue to give their,

Women strong black sons?

Who made peanut butter to spread on bread,

So that their hungry children would eat before going to bed?

Who built the clock so we could tell time?

It was a black man, each and every time.

He built these and other things,

All different sizes and kinds.

Can't you see why they don't want us around?

Because they know that when a black man is up,

 Honey, you can't keep him down!

WHY DO THEY TREAT US BAD?

Why do others treat us so bad?

They give us so much pain and this makes me sad.

Just because my skin is brown, they don't want me and my family around.

God said we should love our neighbors as our brothers,

To get into Heaven, we can do no other.

Why can't we accept each other,

And love one another no matter the color?

Dark skinned people have always been around,

In Biblical days they walked all around town.

I've heard that God is also the color brown.

In the Bible it said Jesus had wooly hair and feet the color of bronze.

Reading that, I now understand why they don't want us around.

People back in the day, did their best to run Jesus out of town,

So really I shouldn't feel too bad, 'cause they don't want me around.

But still it hurts, when people call you names,

And you're the last they pick for childhood games.

In the corporate world, when promotions are given out,

They won't consider a brown man because of some doubt.

But think about this, most things invented,

Came about because of a black man's experience.

Who built houses and didn't get paid?

Whose mother scrubbed floors, because she was a maid?

A black man invented the light bulb stem, the mop, ironing board and iron,

Because he was tired of working so hard.

So when you're feeling bad and suffering from low self-esteem,

Remember Martin Luther King, Jr.

He had a dream that all people, whether they were red, white or blue,

Would love each other as God wanted us to.

So brown skinned people, when others put you down,

Remember the reason they don't want you around.

You have so many skills and great things you can do,

Just believe in yourself because it's really true!

God made us in his image and isn't the color brown in the same family as bronze?

So why should you be hurt,

When your father made the earth,

The people, the land,

The air, sky and sand,

Your face, legs, arms and hands?

Smile, hold your head up high, walk with a long-legged stride,

Because you are special just like they are,

No matter what they say or do, you are special and that is the truth.

LIFE ISSUES

HEADACHES

My head aches so very bad,

It feels like something I've never had.

If I take two aspirins and try to rest,

This is supposed to put me at my best.

But who's to say this method works,

Or will my head continue to hurt?

From stress, diet, or lack of rest,

My body is putting me through a test.

Should I exercise daily and drink plenty of water,

Eat a balanced meal and get plenty of rest?

The doctor said to do all these things and I'd get better,

Then I'd find that my headache just doesn't matter.

WHEN PROBLEMS ARISE

When problems arise and things go wrong,

Remember resolution and conflict management must be strong.

Waiting too long to resolve it,

Won't help those involved one bit.

Cussing, anger, hurt and pain,

Are only symptoms of things that rage will gain.

When someone makes you angry or mad,

Communicate, forgive, let go and live,

As a result you'll become closer comrades.

ONE THING

A strong mind is the one thing we all need.

It helps us live a great life, guaranteed.

Learning new things will help us grow and develop.

Being smart and knowledgeable will allow us to progress together.

What else could help each of us become even better?

YOU'RE WRONG, MY FRIEND!

The problems you have are not meant to last.

The pain you are experiencing will someday be in the past.

But you're wrong, my friend, to blame others for your dilemmas.

Just try to remember when all else fails,

When you're solving a problem,

Look to me, your friend, from January to December.

YOU'RE SPECIAL

You are such a great person.

You are special to each and every one of us.

Your smile is so genuine,

Your compassionate heart,

Makes being around you really smart!

May God continue to guide your precious feet,

To achieve your wildest dreams, whatever they may be.

Remember that having a good heart,

Is certainly one of the keys,

To having positive self-esteem.

God made each of us to be different,

So that we can achieve at our highest percents.

He gave us heart and lots of smarts,

Because from Him,

He hopes we will never really depart.

Ask Him for the things you need,

Pray to Him, get on your knees.

For the kingdom is yours, if you just praise Him.

The Almighty Everlasting King!

STRAIGHT AT YOU

Somebody's looking at you,

Thinking they can see,

You through and through.

Be careful what you say or do,

'Cause others may emulate you.

Admiration, joy and respect for you,

That's exactly what you want folks to do.

Someone is looking straight at you,

Watch out, the finger is pointing, peek-a-boo!!!

SOMETHING STRANGE

I heard something strange today,

About my dog and what she will need,

To stay healthy and strong,

So that she will live long.

But the news broke my heart anyway.

A hysterectomy for my dog.

Oh my! What dialogue?

Removing her ovaries like she is a woman,

Will this give her a longer life span?

So young, never been through a lot in life,

My dog has never been a wife.

Will she miss the things she has never done?

Or will she just continue to be a honey bun?

I don't know about this thing called surgery,

I just feel like, why rush?

What's the hurry?

I GOT ISSUES!

I Got Issues,
So many things my poor heart wishes.
I got issues,
Like unemployment,
Even the military won't represent.
I got issues,
Crying so hard,
I need some tissue,
Don't have no place to live,
'Cause money I don't have to give,
Can't pay my rent or bills,
And my life continues to go downhill.
I got issues,
Don't have no food,
Cause I acted a fool,
Trading my food stamps away for a certain mood,
I got issues,
Drugs, crack and cocaine and other shit that kills,
Dirty, hungry and homeless and feeling so bad,
Wishing hard for things that I never had.
Hey, I got issues
Like so many others,
We've lost our mothers,
For stealing what they worked hard for,
So they threw our asses out the door.

I got issues,

Lost my friends,

'Cause crime, we wouldn't end,

So they said, you're no longer my kin.

I got issues,

Cause help I'm seeking,

With a heart that's speaking,

Begging and pleading,

For me to quit drugs and succeed,

So please, my friends,

Help me to the bitter end!

UNEMPLOYED

Unemployed so long,

All my poor skills gone,

Don't have an education,

Can't enter an occupation,

Can't write or spell,

Thought school was hell,

Don't have nowhere to live,

Because no money I have to give,

Nothing to do,

So I mess with you,

Rob, steal, drink and kill,

Nothing else seems to give me a thrill,

Dying so young,

All my hope is gone,

Because I stayed unemployed,

So damn long!

Rose Jackson-Beavers

WELFARE TO WORK

Welfare to Work makes some clients feel like jerks,

When they only tried to get what they felt they were worth.

Getting a job takes so many skills,

Not only that, but you have to be strong-willed.

When you are classified as a person who wants hand-outs,

People won't listen to you unless you scream and shout.

If only folks knew how it hurts,

To be poor, ignored, talked down to and treated like dirt,

Like I'm not here, but in the Far East,

Like my heart can't break into tiny pieces.

Welfare to Work is supposed to help people like me,

Motivate and give us the skills to become great employees.

But don't just make us feel sad,

Because we chose a life that was bad.

Help us by giving us confidence,

It's the only thing that really makes sense.

Teach, guide and give us a break,

Yes, we'll sometimes make lots of mistakes,

Because we're not perfect, for goodness sake!

Plan activities like you want us around,

Have faith in us and stop putting us down.

Make us feel good about ourselves because we're trying,

After all, we want respect and to be dignifying.

When we find a job after so many attempts,

Don't be too disappointed, if it's only a TEMP!

TRUNK OF LIFE

We live the life we think we can,

Playing bills and raising our kids to a full life span,

With clothes and pictures of our families and special friends,

The trunk of life will hold all our present and future dividends,

With love in our hearts and marriage on our minds,

Dreaming of our future kids who will help to remind,

That we lived a life from the trunk of life,

To help us to leave our footprints to show our past strife.

The things we do and what we say,

Will help our present life go a long way.

So watch your image and keep your smarts,

A child could be watching your very heart.

Present yourself in a very bright light,

Protect yourself both day and night.

So heed this message and do all you can,

To assure you leave a life that's spic and span.

WATCHING YOU

Watching you grow from a baby to a young girl,

Is quite amazing and out of this world.

Constant prayer to keep you healthy, loveable and sweet,

Is something I ask the Lord to allow you to keep.

A lovely smile and a caring heart,

God surely made you a work of art.

Watching you grow from a baby to a young lady,

From a day old to a lady of eighty.

DON'T HAVE!

I don't have a problem with you.

It's just some of the things you say and do.

If you show me respect, like I've shown you,

We'll continue to get along without me dissing you.

So let us treasure the time we have on earth,

By not being mean and spiteful, but full of self-worth.

I TRIED

I tried to talk to my husband today,

About doing something special with his family for the holiday,

But he got upset because he thought we didn't want to visit where he used to stay.

If only he listened to what we had to say,

We would be with him no matter, far or away.

We just wanted to spend a great vacation

With the man we love,

In the Deep South or in the outhouse,

Well, sort of.

WHY IS IT SO HARD?

Why is it so hard to make a man understand,

The problems and pain women experience firsthand?

Why is it so hard to talk to a man about feelings,

When he's the one who thought we were so appealing?

Why is it so hard to love a man who is selfish,

When it is he who wanted her all for himself?

Why is it so hard to question a man,

Without him thinking you're complaining?

Because it is he who has to do the explaining.

All women want are men who listen,

And support them without hesitation,

So that they will feel they have a love,

Built on a strong foundation.

When men and women can sit back and listen to each other,

Then they can be faithful and love one another.

MY HEART HURTS

When my heart hurts and I don't know what to do,

I ask God for help to guide me through.

The sadness I feel and the pain,

And all the other emotions I can't explain.

When my heart hurts and I'm feeling blue,

The tears keep falling because I can't get over you,

And I think, what is a poor woman like me, supposed to do?

One thing that continues to remain true,

When you pray to God, He'll be there for you.

Then suddenly, your broken heart is all brand new.

STREAKS OF LIGHTENING

A streak of lightening flashed across the sky.

It is raining from afar and nearby.

I can see the cars from the opposite side of the highway,

Side by side as our cars pass by.

They can't see my smile or my wave to say goodbye.

A stroke of lightening like a spark in the sky,

So quick and fast, not enough time to ask, " Why?"

Riding through the rain in a covered car,

Looking up at the sky and the beautifully shaped stars.

I can't feel the raindrops because I'm sitting inside.

The beauty so great, I become tongue-tied.

The sky so dark, the moon out of sight,

A night like this you need a flashlight.

I love the rain, but not the thunder and lightening,

It may be okay for adults, but it makes the children frightened.

A rain filled night with raindrops beating on the roof,

Makes my heart tingle and the noise outside soundproof.

A RAIN SLICK NIGHT

A rain slick night while driving on a two-lane highway,

It's terrifying, scary and sometimes nice.

The rain is hitting the window pane,

As the windshield wipers wash as fast as they can.

Ongoing cars in the opposite lanes,

With head lights so bright,

That they light up the night.

The air smelling so fresh and clean,

Fresh rain makes the trees so green,

Why oh why, is the thunder so mean?

On a dark highway, passing through a country town,

Raining so hard, not a soul around.

The other car left, now there is not a sound.

the sky so dark,

The night so blue,

To see through the night,

It will have to take two.

But I won't complain,

Because the rain we all need,

So the farmers can toil and plant,

To have food from their seeds.

BLACK PEARL

I know a girl who has traveled the world,

She is someone of great beauty,

Just like a black pearl, she is rare and unique,

Ultimately beautiful and really neat,

Large in statue but small in frame,

In sports, she put her competitors to shame.

This young lady has lots of game,

Smiling and giving back to her community,

She is loyal, giving others equal opportunity.

Beautiful and rare like a black pearl,

She dreamed success when she was a little girl.

Rare, beautiful, and unique,

Compete against her,

She'll beat you with her technique.

Rare, beautiful and unique,

A black pearl, because this girl,

Jackie Joiner-Kersee, just can't be beat.

DON'T COME

Don't come walking through that door,

With your lips hanging to the floor,

Squinting those little bitty eyes,

'Cause your man told you them lies,

Looking so sad and teary-eyed, you are so worried and so tired.

Nothing is gonna change with you and your man,

Until you yourself leave that madman.

A person will treat you the way you let them,

Disrespecting and mistreating,

Because low self-esteem you were eating.

Stand up, lift your shoulders high,

Tell that man, you need him, it's just a little white lie,

When he is satisfied and you can leave safely,

Get out as fast as you can,

Like a firecracker on the Fourth of July.

ANOTHER MILESTONE

Another milestone you met today,

Struggling and working hard,

You have finally made your way.

Perseverance, determination, and having lots of faith,

Allowed you to see the growth you've made.

Doing something you enjoyed and doing your very best,

Is proof that practice, prayer, and commitment,

Will help you pass any test.

You have achieved great heights,

Because you gave it all your might.

Continue to work hard and be an inspiration to others,

Because each of us should support one another.

Pat yourself on the back and thank God,

Because He never left you and now you can applaud.

Rose Jackson-Beavers

SUMMER DAYS

Hot and humid summer days,

Will melt all your troubles and problems away.

Mosquitoes, flies, knats and bugs,

Will never show your body any love.

They bite and will suck your blood away,

Until your body hurts and then you will say,

Kill that damn bug, kill it today,

Hope that sucker didn't get away!

LOSS OF MY HAIRDRESSER

I lost someone very special today,

It is so painful, because she went away.

I think about all the time she spent,

Teaching me about life's greatest events.

I'll miss the time we shared,

Listening as I sat in her chair.

The knowledge she had about so many things,

Made her one excellent human being.

May God bless and keep her in His care,

Because she was one heck of a person, I declare!

Dedicated to Mayola Williams

SOMETIMES

Sometimes I feel like I just can't go on,

Sometimes I feel so lost and scorn,

Sometimes I feel like a lost, blowing horn.

Sometimes I feel like I just can't get it right,

It doesn't matter if I try with all my might.

Sometimes I feel like I can't trust others,

Sometimes I feel so angry, even with my mother,

About the things in my life,

That I just can't make right.

Sometimes my heart aches with so much pain,

Sometimes I feel like I just won't gain,

The knowledge, the power,

That I need from the Heavenly Father.

Sometimes when I read the Bible, I don't understand,

The message God wants in my hand.

Sometimes I feel like all the rest, the sad,

The angry and the bad.

Sometimes I feel like I'm so great,

Then God turns around and puts me back in place.

Sometimes I feel like I just can't wait,

Sometimes I feel so much hate,

But God, He knows my soul, my heart.

Sumthin' T' Say

He even knows all of my secret thoughts.

Sometimes I need to thank Him again,

And I know God will continue to be my friend.

Sometimes I feel like I'll go to heaven,

But then someone will ruffle my feathers.

Sometimes I act like all the other fellows,

Until I pray and ask the Lord to help me to become better.

Sometimes I study my Bible and pray,

Until I let others lead me astray.

Then I pray, "Lord help me to be better,

To you, my God, my heart I'll give forever."

And one day He will take that sometimes feeling away,

And that is why I pray each and everyday.

ANGER

When you're troubled, hurt and sad,

Don't let others make you so mad.

Anger puts your body through so many emotions,

A quick, beating heart, your blood pressure sky high,

Your hair standing straight and your eyes bucked wide,

You're just too angry; you'll loose your pride.

Don't get so angry that you don't know what to do.

You may end up shooting a person or maybe two!

When you're angry and you just can't think,

Anything can happen as fast as a blink.

You can hurt someone deep down inside,

When all you had to do was keep God by your side.

It's just not worth it to lose self-control,

'Cause when you do,

You're giving the devil your body and your soul.

TROUBLE

Most of the trouble and pain in the world today,

Is due to someone who wouldn't let their anger subside and go away.

They thought too long about what others would say,

Instead of taking the high road and walking away.

They thought others would look down on them,

If they let another brother do them in.

They didn't want to feel embarrassed, rejected or bad,

So the person struck out with the only thing they had.

They used their low self-esteem,

To end someone else's dream.

Just because they couldn't control their anger,

They decided to put others in danger.

By robbing, maiming and killing,

They took another person through something really chilling,

Just because they could not own up to their real feelings.

So remember when you're angry and out of control,

You're just putting your life on hold,

Because when you do someone wrong,

It certainly won't be very long,

Before you go through the same thing, too.

Learn to handle your anger, my friend, get counseling,

And ask God to help, and He will pull you through.

MAKING APPOINTMENTS

Making appointments you know you can't keep,

Is just as bad as falling from a building ten feet.

Don't say you'll be there on time,

When you know,

You will be late for important events.

Being late is as bad as sour lemons,

To one's tongue and one's lips.

The misery and pain of making appointments that are not met,

Can give a hard-working person a reputation,

Of being a disappointment, with a lack of respect.

Try not to be late by setting your clock ahead by ten minutes.

You can believe it will be worth every moment you spent,

Trying to get ready and out of bed early,

Because now you feel relaxed and just downright merry.

TEMPTATION

Temptation is all around,

And it can get you all tied up and bound.

Heartache, trouble and pain,

Running in the streets,

What else would you gain?

Drugs, unemployment, and life threatening diseases,

Are all you'll get when you're out being a tease.

So be wise and avoid temptation, if you please.

For if you succumb to it,

You had better get on your knees,

And pray to God to help you,

And He will, it's guaranteed.

So don't be alarmed,

But take this as a warning,

When temptation comes knocking on your door,

Fall on your knees and get real close to the floor.

Pray morning, evening and night,

God will bless you,

And he'll help you do it right.

GOSSIPING

Gossiping is a very hurtful thing,

It affects me, you and all human beings.

When you spread rumors that aren't true,

You hurt so many people with your low IQ.

Don't say things you know are not true,

Just repeat things that are only about you!

When you spread words that are not true facts,

Before you know it, the words have come right back.

DEATH

Death is very painful for those left behind,

Missing your loved ones and wishing you had more time,

To talk, to listen and make future plans,

By sharing life, joy and talking woman to man.

When death slips in time and time again,

And takes those you love to heaven up above,

It leaves us feeling empty without someone to love.

Death is painful for your family and friends,

Our hearts so broken, it seems they'll never mend.

How much can one take as our hearts continue to break?

What do we need to do, to try to get over you?

Brothers, sisters, parents and friends,

Death is taking everybody, even my very best friend.

But I know one thing, when death comes for me,

I just want to see Jesus the King.

Rose Jackson-Beavers

FEELING BAD

My brother is in the hospital,

And he's feeling pretty bad.

Not only is he hurting, but he's pretty darn sad.

We think he might have cancer,

A disease that's hard to cure.

Unless you pray to God,

To allow you to endure.

Our hearts are filled with pain and concern,

At night we can't sleep, we just toss and turn.

If our brother had a chance to love and learn,

Maybe his body will become healthy again,

It's exactly what his family yearns.

STRESS

Stress can cause much pain and sorrow,

So much trouble for today and tomorrow.

Exercise, rest and eat right,

And take care of yourself with all your might.

If you want to let go of stress,

All you have to do is stay away from that mess,

Like gossiping, fighting and the rest.

Listen, my friend,

When trouble comes and things go wrong,

Get on your knees with a prayer so strong,

God will answer your prayers,

Like you know He will.

Be strong, prayerful and have faith,

He'll answer you,

Just be patient and wait.

CLUTTERED MINDS

A confused and cluttered mind,

Needs more than patience,

It needs time.

To let go of things that are stressful,

And believe in stuff that is pleasant,

Takes more than strength and courage,

It takes growth and maturity into middle age.

Don't let simple things worry you,

Or give you the blahs and the blues,

Life is hard enough and that's my point of view.

Don't clutter your mind with negative sayings,

Because those things can hypnotize you,

And make you believe your mind is through.

Give your mind some peaceful time.

Sit back and let your thoughts recline.

For a healthy mind is a sane mind,

Which only gets better every day with time,

If you just sit back and unwind.

BAD NEWS

Bad news is something you don't want to hear.

It is very painful and takes away your cheer.

When the news you hear is very bleak,

It makes you sad and very weak.

A loved one hurt and filled with sadness,

Is enough to make a sane person go into madness.

Heart so broken and pain so real,

To ease the pain,

You to have to take pain pills.

Bad news affects us all,

In the spring, summer, winter or fall.

No matter the weather,

If it affects God's people,

It really matters.

It doesn't matter your culture or your race,

You can be poor, sad or feeling out of place.

You can have cars, money, homes or great wealth.

You don't care for that, you only want good health.

When someone tells you bad news,

Oh, of course, it may put you in a blue mood.

Just remember, there's always a rainbow after the rain,

And with prayer, you can get over the pain.

Rose Jackson-Beavers

I WANTED TO WRITE

I wanted to write this book to say,

Don't let anybody provoke you,

Just walk away.

Be it small or be it great,

Remember to put on a happy face.

Life is too beautiful,

To sit by and waste.

Just take your pride and go through,

The heavenly gates.

Set your goals, brace your pace.

You can achieve it, if you just don't wait.

You must sacrifice and just have faith.